Guess What!

Student's Book 4

American English

Susannah Reed with Kay Bentley
Series Editor: Lesley Koustaff

CAMBRIDGE
UNIVERSITY PRESS

Contents

Welcome back!

Guess What!

1 [CD1 02] **Listen and point.**

2 [CD1 03] **Listen, point, and repeat.**

3 [CD1 04] **Listen and say the names.**

4 [Think] **Describe and guess who.**

Is it a girl or a boy?   It's a boy.

Does he have dark hair?   No, he doesn't.

Is it Tom?   Yes, it is.

1 dark hair
2 straight hair
3 glasses
4 fair hair
5 curly hair
6 red hair

5 🎵 05 Listen and match. Then sing the song.

1 What does Fred look like?
He's tall, he has blue eyes,
And he has red hair.
He has short red hair.

2 What does Jane look like?
She's tall, she has brown eyes,
And she has straight hair.
She has long straight hair.

3 What does Paul look like?
He's short, he has brown eyes,
And he has dark hair.
He has short dark hair.

6 Look at page 6. Read and match.

1 What does Lucas look like?

a She's tall. She has long straight hair.

2 What does Lily look like?

b He's short. He has brown eyes.

3 What does Tom's sister look like?

c He's tall. He has short fair hair.

4 What does Anna's brother look like?

d She's short. She has red hair.

7 (About Me) Think about your family. Ask and answer.

What does your cousin look like?

She's short, and she has straight dark hair.

Remember!

What does he look like?
He's tall.
He has blue eyes.

8 CD1 06 **Listen and repeat.**

100 cm = 1 m

10 cm 20 cm 30 cm 40 cm 50 cm 60 cm 70 cm 80 cm 90 cm 100 cm

9 CD1 07 **Listen and match. Then ask and answer with a friend.**

a 76 cm
b 1 m, 32 cm
c 91 cm
d 1 m, 67 cm
e 1 m, 19 cm

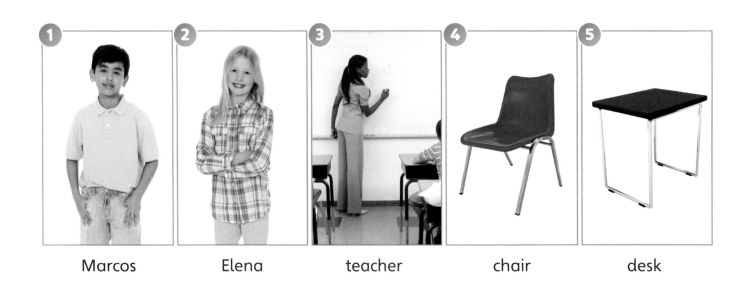

1 Marcos   2 Elena   3 teacher   4 chair   5 desk

How tall is Marcos?   He's 1 meter, 32 centimeters.

How high is the chair?   It's 91 centimeters.

10 About Me **Measure your friends. Then ask and answer.**

How tall are you?   I'm 1 meter, 25 centimeters.

Remember!

100 centimeters =
1 meter

11 CD1 08 **Go to page 102. Listen and repeat the chant.**

Skills: *Reading and speaking*

 Let's start! **What activities do you do with your friends?**

12 **Read and listen. Then match.**

My friends

1 My best friend's name is Rosa. She's very tall. She's 1 meter, 36 centimeters! She has long dark hair, and brown eyes. We like music, and we like playing the recorder together. We have recorder lessons every Wednesday.

2 This is my friend Louis. He has straight dark hair, and green eyes. We're in the same class at school. We like playing Ping-Pong. We play after school on Wednesdays. We like badminton, too.

c

a

b

3 This is me with my friends Sally and James. We like horseback riding. We have riding lessons on Sundays, and we like taking care of the horses, too. Horses are my favorite animals. They're beautiful.

13 **Read again and answer the questions.**

1 How tall is Rosa?
2 Does Rosa have recorder lessons on Sundays?
3 What does Louis look like?
4 What day do Sally and James go horseback riding?

14 **(About Me)** **Think of a friend and answer the questions.**

What's his or her name?
What does he or she look like?
Do you like the same things?
What activities do you do together?

Writing

→ Workbook page 7: Write about a friend and what he or she likes doing.

16 CD1 11 Talk Time **Listen and repeat. Then act.**

watching TV   going ice-skating   making models
playing the guitar   going bowling   playing Ping-Pong

1
What should we do today?
How about watching TV?
OK.

2
What should we do today?
How about playing the guitar?
No, let's go fishing.
OK, good idea.

Say it!

17 CD1 12 **Listen and repeat.**

Owls make no sound when they fly down.

owl

What patterns can you see?

1 CD1 13 Listen and repeat.

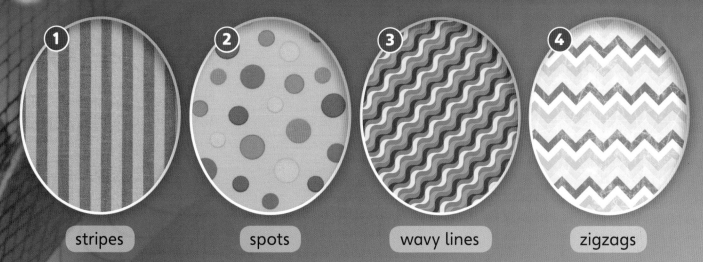

① stripes   ② spots   ③ wavy lines   ④ zigzags

2 Watch the video.

3 What patterns can you see in the pictures?

Guess What!

We all have different patterns of wavy lines on our fingers.

①
②

③
④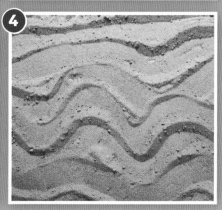

Project

5 Make a mask with different patterns on it.

Look! My mask has lots of green spots next to the eyes. It has wavy lines under the mouth. There are blue zigzags at the top.

4 What patterns do you like drawing?

① Fun sports

Guess What!

1 🎧 CD1 14 **Listen and point.**

2 🎧 CD1 15 **Listen, point, and repeat.**

Adventure vacations

3 🎧 CD1 16 **Listen and answer the questions.**

4 (About Me) **Ask and answer with a friend.**

Do you like skiing?   Yes, I do.

1 fishing
2 ice-skating
3 skateboarding
4 sailing
5 kayaking
6 bowling
7 mountain biking
8 skiing
9 snowboarding

5 🎧 CD1 17 **Listen and choose. Then sing the song.**

1 I'm good at ice-skating/mountain biking,
But I'm not very good at skiing.
Sally isn't good at ice-skating/mountain biking,
But she's very good at skiing.
Sally's a good friend,
But we're good at different things.
Yes! Sally's a good friend,
But we're good at different things.

2 I'm good at snowboarding/skateboarding,
But I'm not very good at sailing.
Ricky isn't good at snowboarding/
skateboarding,
But he's very good at sailing.
Ricky's a good friend,
But we're good at different things.
Yes! Ricky's a good friend,
But we're good at different things.

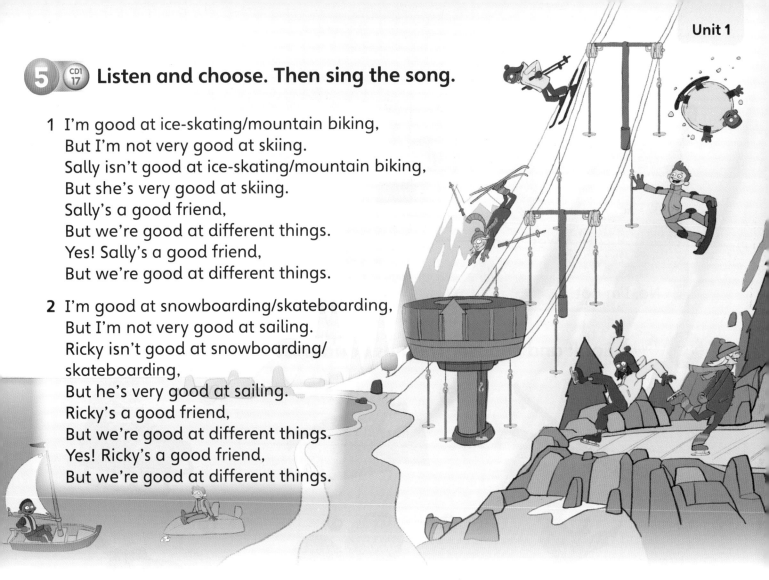

6 (About Me) **Make sentences about you and your friends. Say _true_ or _false_.**

| art | math | music | science |

| skiing | sailing | fishing | ice-skating |

| bowling | snowboarding | mountain biking | kayaking |

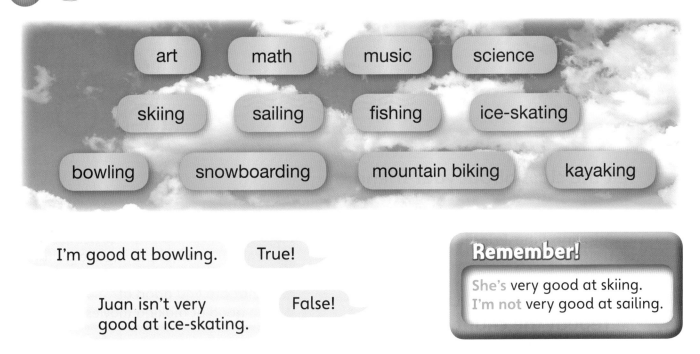

I'm good at bowling.   True!

Juan isn't very   False!
good at ice-skating.

Remember!
She's very good at skiing.
I'm not very good at sailing.

7 (CD1 18) **Listen and repeat.**

1 Are you good at skiing?

Yes, I am.

No, I'm not.

2 What are you good at?

I'm good at ice-skating.

8 (Think) **Look and choose. Then ask and answer with a friend.**

9 **Tell the class about your friend.**

Matthew is good at playing Ping-Pong.

10 (CD1 19) **Go to page 102. Listen and repeat the chant.**

Remember!

Are you good at playing the guitar?
Yes, I am.   No, I'm not.
What are you good at?
I'm good at making movies.

→ Workbook page 14

Skills: *Listening and speaking*

 Let's start! **Do you like talent shows?**

11 CD1 20 **Listen and match.**

Forest School Talent Show!
4:30 this afternoon in the school auditorium.

1 Mel   **2** Kim   **3** Alex

a   b   c

12 CD1 20 **Listen again and answer the questions.**

1 How old is Mel?
2 Is Kim good at making movies?
3 Can Alex play the piano?
4 Who is the winner of the talent show?

13 About Me **Plan a talent show with your friends.**

What are you good at?

I'm good at music. I can play the piano.

I can sing!

Writing

 Workbook page 15: Plan a talent show.

14 Read and listen.

Value: Allow others to work

→ Workbook page 16

15   **Listen and repeat. Then act.**

wash the car   paint a picture   make a movie
write a story   make a cake   sing a song

1
Who wants to make a cake?
I do. I'm good at making cakes.

2
Who wants to paint a picture?
I don't. I'm not good at art.

Say it!

16 Listen and repeat.

Royal pythons coil into balls on the soil.

royal python

What kind of body movements can we make?

1 (CD1 24) Listen and repeat.

1 turn

2 shake

3 bend

4 stretch

5 kick

2 Watch the video.

3 What body movements are the children making in these pictures?

1

2

3

4

Guess What!

We all make the same body movement when we're happy. We smile.

4 What body movements do you make in sports?

Project

5 Write body movements for a street dance.

Movement	Number
Stretch arms and turn	1
Kick	2
Jump	4
Shake your body	4
Kick	2
Stretch arms and turn	1

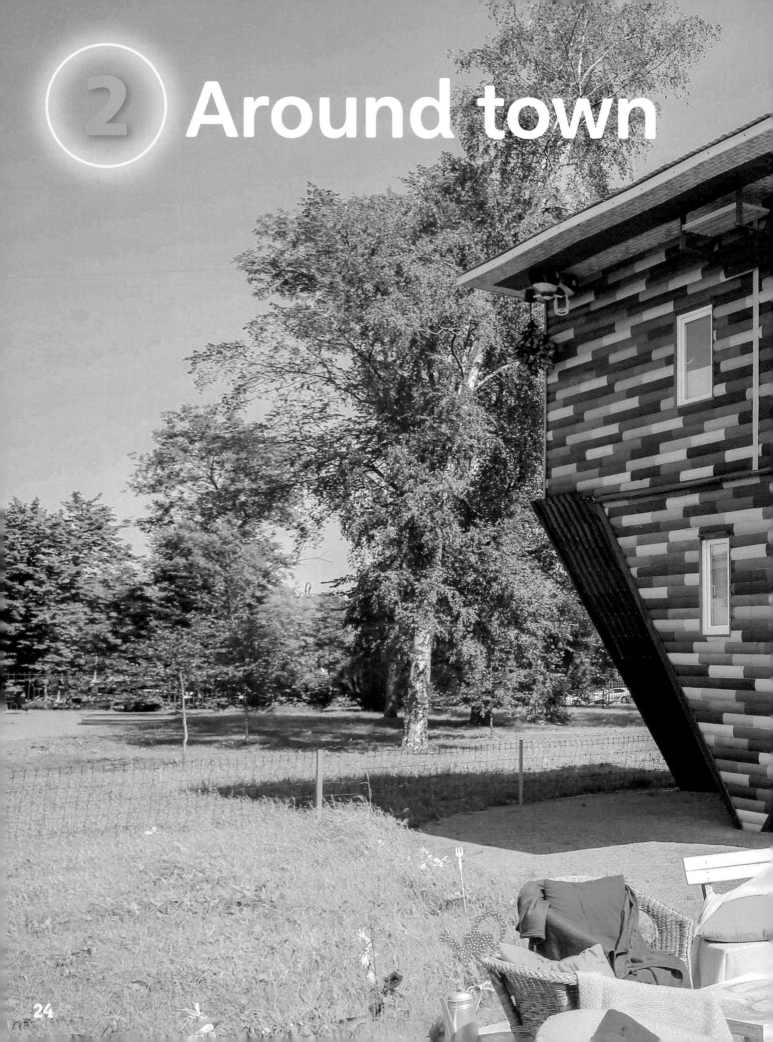

Guess What!

1 (CD1 25) **Listen and point.**

2 (CD1 26) **Listen, point, and repeat.**

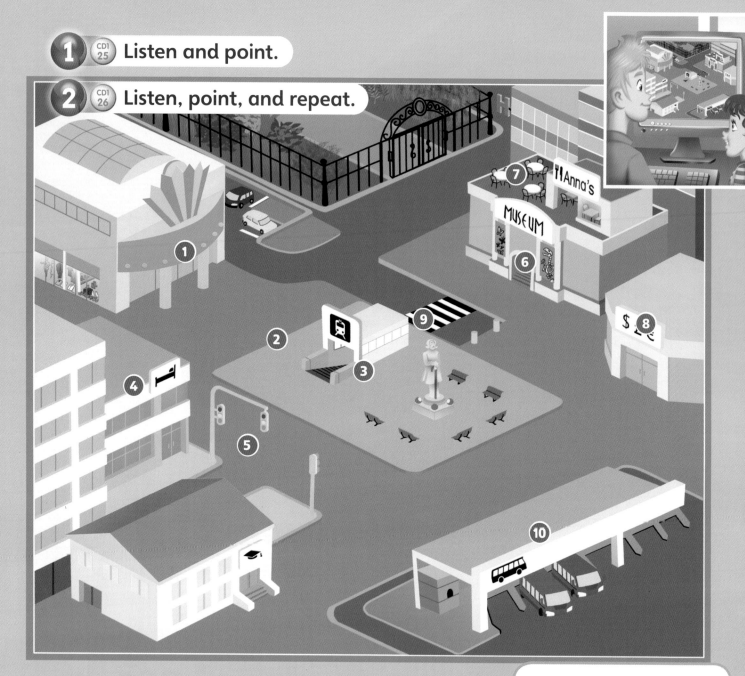

3 (CD1 27) **Listen and say the words.**

4 (Think) **Look at Tom's map. Describe and guess where.**

It's across from the park.   Museum!

1. shopping mall
2. square
3. subway station
4. hotel
5. traffic light
6. museum
7. restaurant
8. bank
9. crosswalk
10. bus station

5 CD1 28 Listen and match. Then sing the song.

1 Where's the museum?
It's in the square.
It's across from the hotel.
Can you see it over there?

2 Where's the subway station?
It's below the square.
It's close to the shopping mall.
Can you see it over there?

3 Where's the plane?
It's above the square.
It's far from the town.
Can you see it up there?

6 Read and match.

1 Where's the museum?	**a**	It's close to the subway station.
2 Where's the plane?	**b**	It's below the square.
3 Where's the shopping mall?	**c**	It's above the square.
4 Where's the subway station?	**d**	It's across from the hotel.

7 (About Me) Make a map of your town. Then ask and answer.

Where's the bank?

It's across from the school.

No, it isn't! It's next to the museum!

Remember!

Where's the bus station?
It's **far from** the hotel.

Listen and repeat.

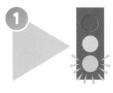
Start!

Go straight ahead.

Turn left.

Turn right.

Stop!

9 CD1 30 **Listen and follow. Then answer.**

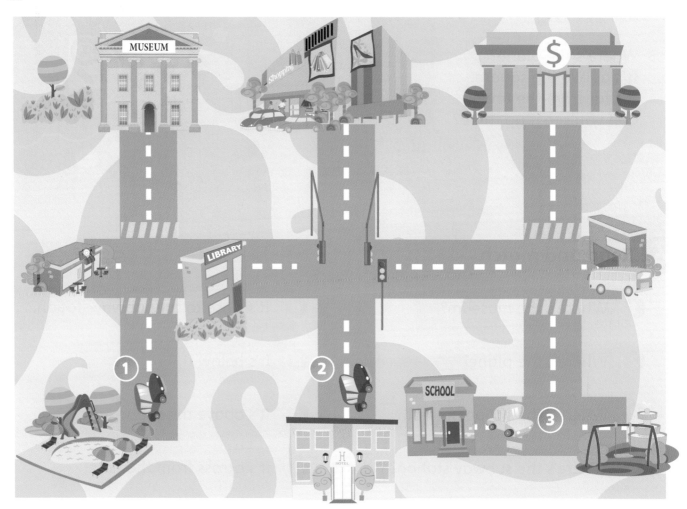

10 Think **Play the game with a friend.**

Start at the restaurant.   Turn left at the crosswalk.

Remember!

Start at the hotel.
Turn right at the library.

11 CD1 31 **Go to page 102. Listen and repeat the chant.**

Skills: *Reading and speaking*

Let's start! What can you see in your town?

12 CD1 32 **Read and listen. Then match.**

a

My trip to London!

Morning ¹ This is London Zoo. It's really big. It's close to my hotel. There are lots of animals in the zoo. This is the giraffe house. Giraffes are my favorite animal.

Lunch ² This is the Rain Forest Café. It's my favorite restaurant in London. What can you see behind the tables? They're elephants!

Afternoon ³ This is the Science Museum. And this is my favorite room – the transportation area. There are lots of cars and a truck. And look above the people. There's a plane!

Evening ⁴ This is Trafalgar Square. There's a big art gallery here. There are statues and a fountain, too.

b

c

d

13 **Read again and choose the words.**

1 London Zoo is close to/far from his hotel.
2 The Rain Forest Café is his favorite shopping mall/restaurant.
3 There's a plane above/below the people in the Science Museum.
4 There's a big art gallery/bus station in Trafalgar Square.

14 (About Me) **Ask and answer with a friend.**

What's your favorite city?
What can you see there?

Writing

→ Workbook page 23: Write about your favourite city.

15 Read and listen.

Value: Cycle safely

→ Workbook page 24

16 **Listen and repeat. Then act.**

library   sports field   shopping mall
supermarket   bus station   museum

1 Excuse me. How do you get to the **bus station**?

Turn left at the crosswalk and go straight ahead.

Thank you.

2 Excuse me. How do you get to the **shopping mall**?

Turn right at the traffic lights and go straight ahead.

Thank you.

Say it!

17 **Listen and repeat.**

Turtles whirl in the surf.

What **3-D shapes** can you see?

1 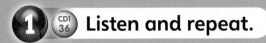 Listen and repeat.

1 sphere 2 cylinder 3 cone 4 cube 5 pyramid

2 Watch the video.

3 What shapes can you see? Read and match.

1 This building is a pyramid shape with glass squares.
2 This building is a cube shape.
3 This building has cylinders at the front.
4 This building is a cone shape.
5 This building has a glass sphere on top.

Some Mexican pyramids are 3,000 years old, but some Egyptian pyramids are 4,000 years old.

Project

5 Make 3-D paper buildings for a town.

4 What shapes can you see in buildings close to your school?

Review Units 1 and 2

1 Find the words in the puzzles and match to the photographs.

fis

boarding

skate

hing

kaya

arding

snowbo

king

Fred

Alice

2 🔊 CD1 37 Listen and say the names.

3 Answer the questions.

1 Where's Fred?
2 What's Josh good at?
3 Is Mia good at skiing?
4 Is Alice in the square?

4 Make your own word puzzles for your friend.

Choose activities or places in town:

super   urant

resta   market

Josh

Mia

→ Workbook pages 28–29

5 **Play the game.**

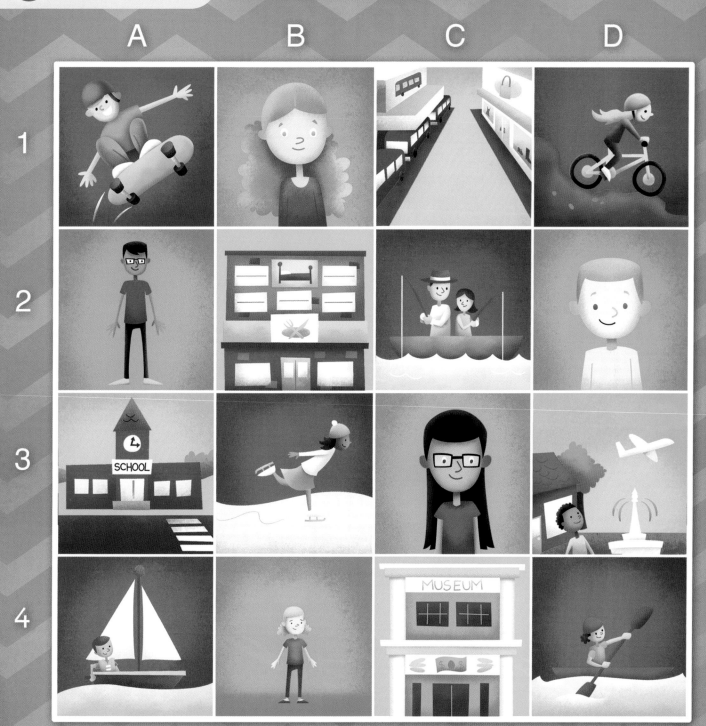

A   B   C   D

Red
Are you good at (skateboarding)?

Blue
What does he/she look like?

Green
Where's the (bus station)?

Number 1. Letter A.   Are you good at skateboarding?   Yes, I am.

35

③ At work

Guess
What!

1  **Listen and point.**

2  **Listen, point, and repeat.**

What do people do?

3  **Listen and say the words.**

4   **Describe and guess who.**

She likes helping people.
She's wearing a white coat.

Doctor!

❶ doctor
❷ nurse
❸ artist
❹ singer
❺ actor
❻ vet
❼ businessman
❽ businesswoman
❾ bus driver
❿ pilot

5 Listen and choose. Then sing the song.

1 What does your aunt do? ...
She's an artist/singer.
Where does she work? ...
She works in a studio.

2 What does your uncle do? ...
He's a bus driver/pilot.
Where does he work? ...
He works on a plane.

3 What does your cousin do? ...
She's a businesswoman/doctor.
Where does she work? ...
She works in an office.

6 Read and match.

1 My dad's a farmer. He works on a farm.

2 My grandma's a teacher. She works in a school.

3 My mom's a train driver. She works on a train.

4 My grandpa's a doctor. He works in a hospital.

a
b
c
d

7 (About Me) Think about your family. Ask and answer.

What does your cousin do?

He's a nurse.

Where does he work?

He works in a hospital.

Remember!

What does your aunt do?
She's an artist.
Where does she work?
She works in a studio.

8 (CD1 42) Listen and repeat.

1.
- What do you want to be?
- I want to be a soccer player.

2.
- Do you want to be a soccer player?
- No, I don't. I want to be a singer.

9 (About Me) Choose what you want to be. Then ask and answer.

10 Tell the class about your friend.

Sally wants to be an actor.

11 (CD1 43) Go to page 102. Listen and repeat the chant.

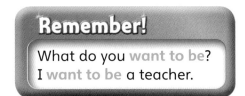

Remember!

What do you want to be?
I want to be a teacher.

→ Workbook page 32

Skills: *Listening and speaking*

Let's start! **Where do you want to work?**

12 (CD1 44) **Listen and match.**

a

b

Sanjay

c

d

Lola

13 (CD1 44) **Listen again and say *true* or *false*.**

1 Sanjay's good at science.
2 Sanjay wants to be a doctor.
3 Lola wants to work in an office.
4 Lola's good at English.

14 **Ask and answer with a friend.**

What are you good at?
Do you want to work with animals or people?
Do you want to work in a school or in an office?

Writing

 Workbook page 33: Write about what you want to be and where you want to work.

→ Workbook page 34

16   **Listen and repeat. Then act.**

give some water to the horse   feed the rabbit   feed the cat
give some milk to the cat   take the dog for a walk

1

Should I take the dog for a walk?

Yes, please.

2

Should I feed the cat?

No, thanks. But you can feed the rabbit.

OK.

Say it!

17   **Listen and repeat.**

Crabs crawl across sand.

crab

→ Workbook page 35

Function: Offering to help   Pronunciation: *cr*   **43**

What kind of
work
is it?

1 🎧 **Listen and repeat.**

outdoors work　　factory work　　transportation work　　store work

2 **Watch the video.**

3 **Look at the pictures. What kind of work can you see?**

Guess What!

We know how old a tree is from the number of circles in its wood.

Project

5 *From trees to stores.* Make a poster.

4 **What kinds of work do you think are difficult?**

Guess! What!

1 (CD1 49) **Listen and point.**

2 (CD1 50) **Listen, point, and repeat.**

3 (CD1 51) **Listen and say the animals.**

4 (Think) **Describe and guess what.**

It's brown, and it can jump. It has a long tail.

Kangaroo!

1 kangaroo
2 koala
3 parrot
4 penguin
5 bat
6 owl
7 jaguar
8 bear
9 panda
10 gorilla

→ Workbook page 38

5 (CD1 52) **Listen and match. Then sing the song.**

1 Gorillas are bigger than pandas,
But gorillas are smaller than bears.
Bears are bigger than gorillas,
And they're bigger than pandas, too.
Animals, animals. Look at the animals!

2 Bats are noisier than koalas,
But bats are quieter than parrots.
Parrots are noisier than bats,
And they're noisier than koalas, too.
Animals, animals. Look at the animals!

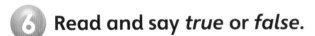

6 **Read and say** *true* **or** *false*.

1 Pandas are smaller than bears.
2 Gorillas are bigger than bears.
3 Bears are bigger than pandas.
4 Bats are noisier than parrots.
5 Koalas are quieter than bats.
6 Parrots are quieter than koalas.

7 (About Me) **Make sentences about your favorite animals. Say** *true* **or** *false*.

Tigers are faster than rabbits.

True!

Remember!

big**ger**
small**er**
nois**ier**
quiet**er**

8 CD1 53 **Listen and repeat.**

1 Are giraffes taller than penguins?

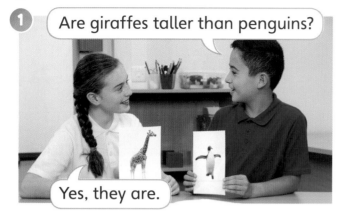

Yes, they are.

2 Are koalas noisier than bears?

No, they aren't.

9 CD1 54 **Listen and answer the questions.**

1	2	3	4
small big	tall short	noisy quiet	slow fast

10 Think **Ask and answer with a friend.**

Are frogs bigger than penguins?   No, they aren't.

11 CD1 55 **Go to page 102. Listen and repeat the chant.**

Remember!

Are parrots quieter than rabbits?
Yes, they are.   No, they aren't.

50 Grammar

→ Workbook page 40

Skills: *Reading and speaking*

 Would you like to work in a zoo?

12 CD1 56 **Read and listen. Then match.**

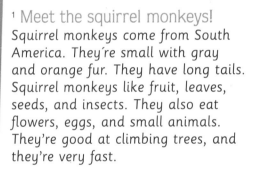

¹ Meet the squirrel monkeys!
Squirrel monkeys come from South America. They're small with gray and orange fur. They have long tails. Squirrel monkeys like fruit, leaves, seeds, and insects. They also eat flowers, eggs, and small animals. They're good at climbing trees, and they're very fast.

² Meet the wallabies!
A wallaby looks like a kangaroo, but it's smaller. Wallabies come from Australia. They eat grass and plants. Wallabies can't run, but they're very good at jumping.

³ Meet our baby red panda!
This is Bo. He's our baby red panda! Red pandas come from Asia. They're red and brown, and they have long tails. Red pandas eat lots of things. They like plants, insects, eggs, birds, and small animals!

13 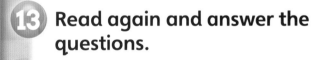 **Read again and answer the questions.**

1 Can squirrel monkeys climb trees?
2 What do wallabies eat?
3 Do red pandas eat meat?
4 Which animal comes from Australia?

14 About Me **Ask and answer with a friend.**

What's your favorite wild animal?
What does it look like?
Where does it come from?
What does it eat?

Writing

➡ 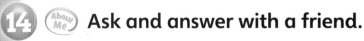 Workbook page 41: Write about your favorite animal.

15 CD2 02 Read and listen.

Value: Take care of nature

→ Workbook page 42

16 CD2 03 **Listen and repeat. Then act.**

kite   eraser   glue   balls   colored markers   scissors

1
Where's the glue?
It's here.
Can you pass it, please?
Yes, of course.

2
Where are the scissors?
They're here.
Can you pass them, please?
Yes, of course.

Say it!

17 CD2 04 **Listen and repeat.**

Frogs catch fruit flies with their tongues.

frog

What animal group is it?

1 CD2 05 Listen and repeat.

mammals

reptiles

amphibians

2 Watch the video.

3 What animal group is it? Read and match.

1 It's an amphibian. It can live on land and in water.
2 It's a bird, and it can fly.
3 It's a fish, and it can swim.
4 It's a mammal. It has spots on it, and it can climb.
5 It's a reptile, and it can walk and swim.

Guess What!

The hummingbird is the only bird that can fly backward.

Project

5 Make a mind map with the five animal groups.

4 What group of animals would you like to film?

→ Workbook page 44

Review Units 3 and 4

1 Find the words in the puzzles and match to the photographs.

v*t

p*l*t

s*ng*r

*rt*st

2 CD2 06 Listen and say the letters.

3 Read and answer the questions.

1 Look at picture a.
  What does she do?

2 Look at picture b.
  Where does she work?

3 Look at picture c.
  Is the sculpture bigger
  or smaller than the artist?

4 Look at picture d.
  Does he work on a plane?

4 Make your own word puzzles for your friend.

> Choose jobs or wild animals:
> k*ng*r**
> g*r*ll*

→ Workbook pages 46–47

5 **Play the game.**

Finish

14

15 tall?

16 25×3=

13

4

5 doctor / hospital?

12 small?

3 big?

6 quiet?

11 pilot / plane?

2 farmer / office?

1

Start

7

10

9 slow?

8 businessman / studio?

Red
Do you want to be a (doctor)?

Blue
Does (a farmer) work in (an office)?

Yellow
Are (gorillas) (bigger) than (rabbits)?

57

Food and drink

Guess
What!

1 (CD2 07) **Listen and point.**

2 (CD2 08) **Listen, point, and repeat.**

3 (CD2 09) **Listen and answer the questions.**

4 (Think) **Describe and guess who.**

He wants pasta for lunch.   Tom!

1. pasta
2. yogurt
3. soup
4. pizza
5. salad
6. nuts
7. tea
8. coffee
9. cookie
10. chips

5 **Listen and choose. Then sing the song.**

1 I always have a sandwich/pizza for lunch,
And I usually have some fruit.
Sometimes I have yogurt/soup,
But I never have cookies or chips.
No, he never has cookies or chips!

2 I usually have pasta/salad for dinner,
And sometimes I have some soup.
I always have some vegetables/fruit,
But I never have cookies or chips.
No, he never has cookies or chips!

He never has cookies or chips!

6 (Think) **Look at the song. Then read and correct the sentences.**

1 I never have a sandwich for lunch.
2 I always have pasta for dinner.
3 Sometimes I have chips for lunch.
4 I never have vegetables for dinner.
5 I always have cookies for dinner.

Number 1. He always has a sandwich for lunch.

always

usually

sometimes

never

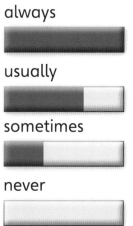

7 (About Me) **Make sentences and say *true* or *false*.**

I always have chips for lunch.

False!

Remember!
I **always have** vegetables for dinner.
He **never has** cookies for dinner.

8 CD2 11 **Listen and repeat.**

9 (About Me) **Make questions. Then ask and answer with a friend.**

How often do you have

for breakfast?

for lunch?

for dinner?

10 **Tell the class about you and your friend.**

Pablo has toast for breakfast every day. I usually have yogurt.

11 CD2 12 **Go to page 103. Listen and repeat the chant.**

Remember!

How often do you have vegetables for lunch?
Every day. Usually. Sometimes. Never.

Skills: *Listening and speaking*

 What do you usually have for lunch?

12 CD2 13 **Listen and match.**

Grace

a

Monday	Tuesday	Wednesday	Thursday
pizza	pasta	soup	sandwich
salad	vegetables	salad	salad
fruit	yogurt	yogurt	fruit
yogurt	water	water	yogurt
water			water

Louis

b

Monday	Tuesday	Wednesday	Thursday
sandwich	chicken	soup	pasta
salad	salad	salad	vegetables
fruit	fruit	yogurt	fruit
yogurt	nuts	fruit	juice
water	juice	water	

13 CD2 13 **Listen again and answer the questions.**

1 How often does Grace have salad for lunch?
2 Does Grace sometimes have pizza?
3 How often does Louis have nuts?
4 Does Louis like yogurt?

14 About Me **Ask and answer with a friend.**

Do you always have a healthy lunch?
Do you usually have fruit, vegetables, or salad?
What do you never have for lunch?

Writing

 Workbook page 51: Make a lunch diary and write about it.

15 CD2 14 **Read and listen.**

1 Week 5 We need bean bags.

$15! That's a lot of money.

How can we get $15?

$15

2

3 How about selling fruit?

I can give you $10 to buy the fruit.

Thanks, Dad!

4 Let's wash our hands first.

Good idea. Come on, Anna.

OK.

5 We have fruit salad ...

... and orange juice.

Great!

6 How much is the fruit salad?

It's one dollar.

Can I have two, please?

Yes, of course. Here you are.

$1

7 28, 29, 30, 31, 32 dollars. Wow!

We can buy two bean bags!

64   Value: Be clean around food

→ Workbook page 52

16   **Listen and repeat. Then act.**

| tea | orange juice | pizza | cookies | chips | nuts |

1

$1.30
Extra shot $0.25
Syrup shot $0.25

It's one dollar.

How much is the orange juice?

Can I have two, please?

Yes, of course.

2

Hot chocolate
Americano $0.75
Fairtrade tea

Specialty teas

How much are the cookies?

They're fifty cents.

Can I have three, please?

Yes, of course.

Say it!

17 **Listen and repeat.**

Aardvarks come out in the dark.

aardvark

Function: Shopping   Pronunciation: *ar*   **65**

Where does **water** come from?

1 (CD2 17) **Listen and repeat.**

1. rain
2. glacier
3. well
4. spring

2 **Watch the video.**

3 **What can you see in the pictures?**

1

2

3

4

4 **Where are the big rivers in your country?**

Guess What!

About 60% of our body is made up of water.

Project

5 **Make a shape poem about where water comes from.**

Water falling, falling from the clouds. Rain comes down into the rivers and oceans. Water, water all around from the wells and springs in the ground.

water falling
from the clouds
into the ground
springs and wells
water running into
rivers and the ocean

6 Health matters

Guess
What!

1 CD2 18 **Listen and point.**

2 CD2 19 **Listen, point, and repeat.**

3 CD2 20 **Listen and answer the questions.**

4 Think **Describe and guess who.**

He has a cold.   Tom!

1 cold
2 cough
3 earache
4 stomachache
5 backache
6 sore throat
7 temperature
8 toothache
9 headache

5 (CD2 21) **Listen and match. Then sing the song.**

1 Oh, dear, what's the matter?
What's the matter with you, Tim?
I have a headache.
Oh, dear, poor you!

2 Oh, dear, what's the matter?
What's the matter with Max?
He has a stomachache.
Oh, dear, poor him!

3 Oh, dear, what's the matter?
What's the matter with Mary?
She has a cough and a cold.
Oh, dear, poor her!

6 (CD2 22) **Now listen and say the names.**

7 (Think) **Play a mime game.**

What's the matter with Charlie?

He has a stomachache.

Do you have a stomachache?

Yes, I do.

Remember!

What's the matter?
I have a cough and a cold.

8 (CD2 23) **Listen and repeat.**

Can you go sailing today?

No, I can't. I have a sore throat and a temperature.

9 (CD2 24) **Listen and match.**

1

2

3

4

a

b

c

d

10 (Think) **Ask questions and say why you can't.**

Can you go ice-skating today?

No, I can't. I have an earache.

11 (CD2 25) **Go to page 103. Listen and repeat the chant.**

Remember!

Can you play basketball today?
No, I can't. I have a cough and a cold.

Skills: *Reading and speaking*

 How often do you have a cold?

12 (CD2 26) **Read and listen. Then match.**

Do you have a cold?

Make some lemon and honey! Lemon and honey is a very healthy drink. It's good for colds, and it's easy to make! Try this simple recipe at home.

1 You need a lemon, some honey, and some hot water.
2 Cut the lemon. Squeeze the juice into a cup.
3 Add some honey.
4 Add the hot water. Be careful! An adult can help.

It's ready! Now sit down and enjoy your lemon and honey!

13 **Read again and say *true* or *false*.**

1 Lemon and honey is a healthy drink.
2 It isn't good for colds.
3 It's difficult to make.
4 You need hot water for the drink.

14 (About Me) **Ask and answer with a friend.**

What healthy foods and drinks can you make?
Can you make a salad?
Can you make a fruit salad?
Can you make orange juice?
Can you make a sandwich?

Writing

→  Workbook page 59: Write a recipe for a healthy food or drink.

1 Week 6
We need skateboards.

Let's ask our cousin Chris!

He goes to skateboarding club today.

2

3 Skateboarding competition today Win a skateboard!

It's a competition!

Go, Chris!

4 Oh, dear!

Are you OK, Chris?

Yes, I think so. My leg hurts, but I'm OK. Don't worry.

5 Do you have a headache, Chris?

No, I'm OK now.

But where's your skateboard?

6 Skateboarding competition today Win a skateboard!

Max!

He's really good!

7 Good job, Max!

Sorry, Chris!

That's OK! I'm good at skateboarding, but Max is very good!

1

74 Value: Be a good sport

→ Workbook page 60

16   **Listen and repeat. Then act.**

backache earache headache temperature sore throat cough

1

Are you OK?

Yes, I think so. Don't worry.

Oh, good!

2

Are you OK?

No, I don't think so. I have a headache.

Oh, dear!

Say it!

17 **Listen and repeat.**

Spiders spin special webs.

spider

What can we use plants for?

1 (CD2 30) **Listen and repeat.**

1

fabric

2

fuel

3

medicine

2 **Watch the video.**

3 (CD2 31) **Listen and say what picture it is.**

1

2

3

4

5

Guess What!

Some bamboo plants can grow almost one meter in a day.

Project

5 Make a poster to show what plants are used for.

4 **Can you think of something new you could make from a plant?**

Review Units 5 and 6

1 Find the words and match to the photographs.

pizzalpastapsaladesoup

2 (CD2 32) Listen and say the names.

3 Read and say the names.

1 She likes making salad.
2 He sometimes makes pizza.
3 He likes making soup.
4 She often makes pasta with chicken and vegetables.

4 Make your own word puzzle for your friend.

Choose food or health:
toothachebcoughocold

Joe

Will

Rosie

Sara

→ Workbook pages 64–65

5 **Play the game.**

Start

1. breakfast?
2. dinner?
3. You have a headache! **Go back one!**
4. lunch?
5. breakfast?
6. You have an earache! **Go back one!**
7. dinner?
8. lunch?
9. You have a temperature! **Go back one!**
10. breakfast?
11. dinner?
12. You have a cough! **Go back one!**
13. lunch?
14. breakfast?
15. You have a stomachache! **Go back one!**
16. dinner?

Finish

I never have pizza for breakfast!

How often do you have pasta for dinner? Every day.

7 Buildings

Guess What!

81

1 (CD2 33) **Listen and point.**

2 (CD2 34) **Listen, point, and repeat.**

3 (CD2 35) **Listen and answer the questions.**

4 (Think) **Describe and guess where.**

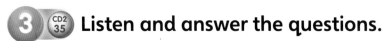

There are lots of old toys here.

Attic!

1 first floor		**6** roof
2 second floor		**7** basement
3 third floor		**8** garage
4 fourth floor		**9** stairs
5 elevator		**10** attic

5 CD2 36 **Listen and choose. Then sing the song.**

1 Where were you yesterday?
Where were you yesterday morning?
I was in the kitchen/living room,
In my apartment on the third floor.

2 Where were you yesterday?
Where were you yesterday afternoon?
I was in the living room/bedroom,
In my apartment on the third floor.

3 Where were you yesterday?
Where were you yesterday evening?
I was in the roof garden/attic,
Above my apartment on the third floor.
My apartment on the third floor.
The third floor. The third floor.

 6 CD2 37 **Listen and say the names.**

John   Marta   Leon   Lola

 7 About Me **Ask and answer with a friend.**

Where were you yesterday morning?

I was at home. I was in the living room.

Remember!

Where were you yesterday morning?
I was in the kitchen.

8  **Listen and repeat.**

Were you at home last night?

No, I wasn't. I was at the movies.

Yes, I was.

Were you at home?

9 (Think) **Make questions. Ask and answer with a friend.**

Questions

| Were you | at home
at school
at the movies
at a restaurant
on the bus
in the hospital
at a shopping mall
at the swimming pool | yesterday morning?
yesterday afternoon?
yesterday evening?
last night? |

10 (About Me) **Play a guessing game.**

Were you in the hospital last night?

No, I wasn't. Guess again.

11 **Go to page 103. Listen and repeat the chant.**

Remember!

Were you at home last night?
Yes, I was.   No, I wasn't.

Skills: *Listening and speaking*

 Who's your favorite singer?

12 (CD2 40) **Look at Misha's diary. Listen and choose.**

Misha

Saturday

<u>Morning</u>
at home / in a hotel / at a
shopping mall

<u>Lunch</u>
in a restaurant / at home /
at a park

<u>Afternoon</u>
at home / in the recording
studio / at the movie theater

<u>Evening</u>
in a hotel / at home / at a
concert

13 (CD2 40) **Listen again and answer the questions.**

1 Where was Misha in the morning?
2 Where was she at lunch?
3 Where was she in the afternoon?
4 Where was she in the evening?

14 (About Me) **Ask and answer with a friend.**

Where were you on Saturday morning?
Where were you on Sunday afternoon?
Were you at the park on Saturday?
Were you at a concert on Saturday evening?

Writing

→ Workbook page 69: Choose one day. Where were you? Write a diary for that day.

16 (Talk Time) **Listen and repeat. Then act.**

Grandpa   Ben   Jane   Grandma   Lara   Uncle John

1

Hello?

Hello, it's Sam. Is Jane there, please?

Yes, she is. Just a minute.

Thank you.

2

Hello?

Hello, it's Sally. Is Grandpa there, please?

No, I'm sorry, he isn't.

OK, thank you. Goodbye.

Say it!

17 CD2 43 **Listen and repeat.**

Black ducks stand on rocks.

black duck

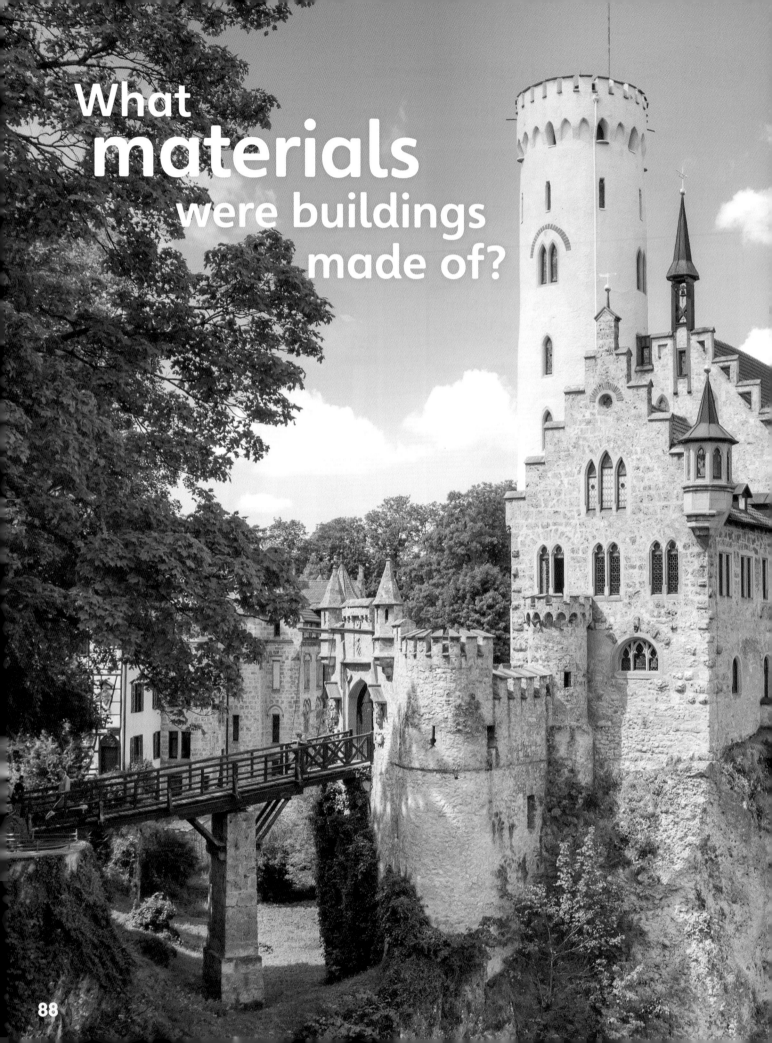

What materials were buildings made of?

1 **CD2 44** **Listen and repeat.**

1

clay

2

stone

3

animal skins

2 **Watch the video.**

3 **What are these buildings made of?**

1
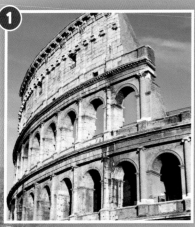

2

3

4

Guess What!

Animal skins were used for water bottles in the eighth century.

Project

5 **Make a fact file about an old building in your country.**

Building: castle
Country: Spain
Material: stone

This is Santa Catalina Castle. It has lots of windows, but they're very small. In this beautiful castle there's a hotel and a swimming pool!

4 **What different things are made of stone?**

8 Weather

Guess What!

1 (CD2 45) Listen and point.

2 (CD2 46) Listen, point, and repeat.

Today's weather

Temperature

Weather

1 hot
2 sunny
3 cold
4 warm
5 snowy
6 cloudy
7 foggy
8 windy
9 rainy

3 (CD2 47) Listen and say the numbers.

4 (About Me) Ask and answer with a friend.

Do you like cold weather?   No, I don't. I like hot weather.

→ Workbook page 74

5 Listen and match. Then sing the song.

1 What was the weather like yesterday?
It was cold and rainy.
What's the weather like today?
It's hot and sunny.
Today it's hot and sunny.
So we can go out and play.
Hooray!

2 What was the weather like yesterday?
It was cold and foggy.
What's the weather like today?
It's cold and snowy.
Today it's cold and snowy.
So we can go out and play.
Hooray!

 6 Listen and answer the questions.

yesterday morning

yesterday afternoon

yesterday evening

last night

 7 Ask and answer with a friend. Say *true* or *false*.

What was the weather like yesterday?

It was cold and snowy.

False! It was cold and rainy.

Remember!

It was cold and rainy yesterday.
It's hot and sunny today.

8 (CD2 50) **Listen and repeat.**

1 Was it cloudy on Monday?

No, it wasn't. It was hot and sunny.

2 Was it rainy on Saturday?

Yes, it was.

9 (CD2 51) **Look at the weather diary. Listen and answer the questions.**

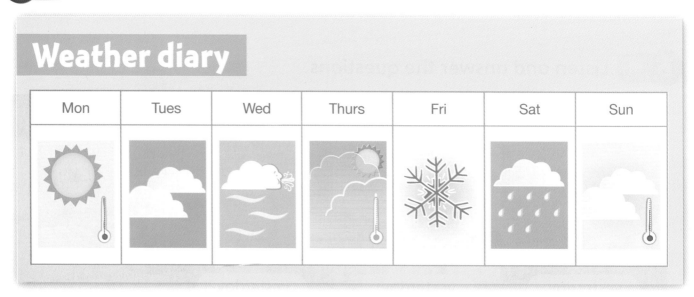

Weather diary

Mon	Tues	Wed	Thurs	Fri	Sat	Sun

10 (About Me) **Make a weather diary. Ask and answer with a friend.**

Was it hot and sunny on Saturday?

No, it wasn't. It was cold and rainy.

11 (CD2 52) **Go to page 103. Listen and repeat the chant.**

Remember!

Was it hot and sunny on Monday?
Yes, it was.   No, it wasn't.

Skills: *Reading and speaking*

Is it snowy in your country?

12 CD2 53 **Read and listen. Then match.**

Hi Kalu,

1 How are you? I'm fine. It was my birthday on Saturday. I'm eleven now. My birthday was great. It was a cold and snowy day, and I was at the Sapporo Snow Festival with my family.

2 The snow festival is every year in February. It's fantastic. It's really big, and there are lots of amazing snow sculptures. This is a photograph of my favorite snow sculpture this year. Can you see what it is? It's a snow building.

3 There are also snow animals and lots of snowmen and snow women. This is a snow family!

4 The snow festival is beautiful at night, too. What's your favorite festival?

Email me soon.

Best wishes,

Yasuko

13 Read and say *true* or *false*.

1 Yasuko's birthday was on Sunday.
2 Yasuko was at the snow festival with her friends.
3 The snow festival is every April.
4 Yasuko likes the snow festival.
5 You can see lots of snow sculptures at the festival.

14 About Me **Ask and answer with a friend.**

When's your birthday?
What festivals do you have in your country?
What's your favorite festival?

Writing

→ Workbook page 77: Write about your favorite festival.

15 CD2 54 **Read and listen.**

1 Adventure Playground

Good job, everyone!
Our Adventure Playground is ready!
Please come to the opening party
on Saturday at four o' clock.

2 It's Saturday today!

What time does the party start?

At four o'clock.

Hurry up, we're late!

3 Adventure Playground

Welcome, everyone, and thank you for your hard work!

I want to be on TV!

4 The Adventure Playground is now open!

5 Wow! This is fantastic.

Faster!

Look! There's an owl.

Value: Work hard and try your best

→ Workbook page 78

16   **Listen and repeat. Then act.**

> TV program   talent show   movie   snow festival
> birthday party   swimming competition

1 When does the movie start?
At five o'clock.
Hurry up! We're late.

2 What time does the birthday party start?
OK, we have time.
At seven thirty.

Say it!

17  **Listen and repeat.**

Elands eat grass and are land animals.

eland

What's the weather like around the world?

1 CD2 57 Listen and repeat.

hurricane

tornado

rainstorm

blizzard

thunder and lightning

2 Watch the video.

3 What's the weather like? Read and match.

1 This weather's snowy and very cold.
2 It's a cone-shaped storm above the land.
3 This weather's cloudy and very rainy.
4 After we see this, it's very noisy.
5 It goes above the ocean, then on the land. It has an eye.

Guess What!

The middle of a hurricane is called its eye.

1
2
3
4
5

Project

5 Make a weather chart for your country.

Months	Weather	
January	rainy	
February	cold	
March	snowy	
April	sunny	
May	rainy	
June	warm	
July	rainstorm	
August	thunder and lightning	
September	hurricane	
October	foggy	
November	snowy	
December	cold	

4 What kind of weather would you like to write about in a story?

Review   Units 7 and 8

1 Find the words and match to the photographs.

ysown

nusny

yiran

dinwy

a

b

2 CD2 58 Listen and say the letters.

3 Read and answer.

1 Look at picture a. What was the weather like?

2 Look at picture b. Was it sunny?

3 Look at picture c. Where was she?

4 Look at picture d. Was he at the beach?

c

d

4 Make your own word puzzles for your friend.

Choose weather or places in a building:
orof tiasrs mbtaense

→ Workbook pages 82–83

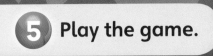

5 Play the game.

Yesterday at twelve thirty …

Mrs. Long

Lucy

Mr. Long

Miles

Player 1

1 Was it windy?
2 Was it hot?
3 Where was the cat?
4 Where was the gorilla?
5 Was the bike in the garage?
6 Was Lucy in the attic?

Player 2

1 Was it snowy?
2 Was it cold?
3 Where was the dog?
4 Where was the penguin?
5 Was the parrot in the kitchen?
6 Was Miles in the basement?

Chants

Welcome back! (page 8)

 Listen and repeat the chant.

Ten, twenty, thirty,
Forty, fifty, sixty,
Seventy, eighty, ninety,
And one hundred!
I can count to one hundred.

Ten, twenty, thirty,
Forty, fifty, sixty,
Seventy, eighty, ninety,
And one hundred!
I can count to one hundred.

Unit 1 (page 18)

 Listen and repeat the chant.

Are you good at skiing?
Yes, I am. Yes, I am.
What are you good at?
I'm good at skiing.

Are you good at ice-skating?
No, I'm not. No, I'm not.
What are you good at?
I'm good at roller-skating.

Unit 2 (page 28)

 Listen and repeat the chant.

Start at the traffic lights!
Go straight ahead.
Turn left at the bank.
Stop! Stop! Stop!

Start at the traffic lights!
Go straight ahead.
Turn right at the park.
Stop! Stop! Stop!

Unit 3 (page 40)

 Listen and repeat the chant.

What do you want to be?
I want to be a singer.
Do you want to be a singer?
Yes, I do. Yes, I do.

Do you want to be a teacher?
No, I don't. No, I don't.
I want to be a doctor.
George wants to be a doctor.

Unit 4 (page 50)

  Listen and repeat the chant.

Are giraffes taller than penguins?
Yes, they are. Yes, they are.
Are koalas noisier than bears?
No, they aren't. No, they aren't.

Are snakes longer than crocodiles?
Yes, they are. Yes, they are.
Are frogs bigger than owls?
No, they aren't. No, they aren't.

Unit 5 (page 62)

 Listen and repeat the chant.

How often do you have salad for lunch?
Every day. Every day.
I have salad for lunch every day.
He has salad for lunch every day.

How often do you have toast for breakfast?
Never. Never. Never.
I never have toast for breakfast.
She never has toast for breakfast.

Unit 6 (page 72)

 Listen and repeat the chant.

Can you go sailing today?
No, I can't. No, I can't.
I have a sore throat and a temperature.
Oh, dear! A sore throat and a temperature.

Can you play basketball today?
No, I can't. No, I can't.
I have a cough and a cold.
Oh, dear! A cough and a cold.

Unit 7 (page 84)

 Listen and repeat the chant.

Were you at home last night?
Yes, I was. Yes, I was.
I was at home.

Were you at home last night?
No, I wasn't. No, I wasn't.
I was at the movies.

Unit 8 (page 94)

 Listen and repeat the chant.

Was it hot and sunny on Monday?
Yes, it was. Yes, it was.
It was hot and sunny.

Was it hot and sunny on Tuesday?
No, it wasn't. No, it wasn't.
It was cloudy.

Thanks and Acknowledgments

Many thanks to everyone in the excellent team at Cambridge University Press. In particular we would like to thank Emily Hird, Liane Grainger, and Camilla Agnew whose professionalism, enthusiasm, experience, and talent makes them all such a pleasure to work with.

We would also like to give special thanks to Lesley Koustaff for her unfailing support, expert guidance, good humor, and welcome encouragement throughout the project.

The authors and publishers would like to thank the following contributors:
Blooberry Design: concept design, cover design, book design, page makeup
Christine Barton: editing
Ann Thomson: art direction, picture research
Gareth Boden: commissioned photography
Lisa Hutchins: freelance editing
Ian Harker: audio recording
Robert Lee, Dib Dib Dub Studios: song and chant composition
Vince Cross: theme tune composition
James Richardson: arrangement of theme tune
John Marshall Media: audio recording and production
Phaebus: video production
hyphen S.A.: publishing management, American English edition

The authors and publishers acknowledge the following sources of copyright material and are grateful for the permissions granted. Although every effort has been made, it has not always been possible to identify the sources of all the material used or to trace all copyright holders.

If any omissions are brought to our notice, we will be happy to include the appropriate acknowledgments on reprinting.

The authors and publishers would like to thank the following illustrators:
Pablo Gallego (Beehive Illustration) 5, 6, 10, 15, 16, 25, 26, 30, 37, 38, 42, 47, 48, 52, 59, 60, 64, 69, 70, 74, 81, 82, 86, 91, 92, 96; Luke Newell 7, 17, 27, 39, 49, 61, 71, 83, 93; A Corazon Abierto (Sylvie Poggio Artists) 18, 28, 40, 94; Marcus Cutler (Sylvie Poggio Artists) 35, 57, 79, 101

The authors and publishers would like to thank the following for permission to reproduce photographs:

p.2–3: Tatiana Popova/Shutterstock; p.4–5: Yi Lu/Viewstock/Corbis; p.8 (1), p.8 (2): Johnny Greig/Getty Images; p.8 (3): OJO Images Ltd/Alamy; p.8 (4): Bejim/Shutterstock; p.8 (5): Sergey Pavlov/Getty Images; p.9 (B/G): Iakov Kalinin/Shutterstock; p.9 (a): Kuttig – People/Alamy; p.9 (b): Datacraft – Sozaijiten/Alamy; p.9 (c), p.50 (3): Juniors Bildarchiv GmbH/Alamy; p.11 (B/G), p.87 (B/G): Robert Harding Picture Library Ltd/Alamy; p.11 (BR): All Canada Photos/Alamy; p.12–13: Thierry GRUN/Alamy; p.13 (T-1): Daniela Pelazza/Shutterstock; p.13 (T-2): Jani Bryson/Getty Images; p.13 (T-3): Philippe Intraligi/Ikon Images/Corbis; p.13 (T-4): MT511/Shutterstock; p.13 (CL): irin-k/Shutterstock; p.13 (CR): Moiz Husein Dossaji/Shutterstock; p.13 (BL): Photoshot Holdings Ltd/Alamy; p.13 (BC): Jiri Vaclavek/Shutterstock; p.14–15: mediacolor's/Alamy; p.17 (B): Pakhnyushchy/Shutterstock; p.19 (B/G): Lora liu/Shutterstock; p.19 (TL): Sean Justice/Shutterstock; p.19 (TC): Nikoncharly/Getty Images; p.19 (TR): Digital Vision/Getty Images; p.21 (B/G), p.65 (B/G), p.97 (B/G): David Cayless/Getty Images; p.21 (BR): SuperStock/Alamy; p.22: Mira/Alamy; p.23 (T-1): I love images/Getty Images; p.23 (T-2): Thomas Perkins/Getty Images; p.23 (T-3): Image Source Plus/Alamy; p.23 (T-4): J and J Productions/Getty Images; p.23 (T-5): Chris Stein/Getty Images; p.23 (CL): Radius Images/Alamy; p.23 (CR): Amy Myers/Shutterstock; p.23 (BL): @Michi B./Getty Images; p.23 (BC): F1online digitale Bildagentur GmbH/Alamy; p.24–25: Andrey Pronin/ZUMA Press/Corbis; p.29 (B/G): QQ7/Shutterstock; p.29 (T): Greg Williams/REX; p.29 (C): tim gartside london/Alamy; p.29 (BL): Imagestate Media Partners Limited – Impact Photos/Alamy; (BR): Michael Kemp/Alamy; p.31 (B/G), p.43 (B/G): Barry Downard/Getty Images; p.31 (BR): Mauricio Handler/Getty Images; p.32: Zoonar GmbH/Alamy; p.33 (T-1): Dan Kosmayer/Shutterstock; p.33 (T-2): Laborant/Shutterstock; p.33 (T-3): GeorgeMPhotography/Shutterstock; p.33 (T-4): poparctic/Shutterstock; p.33 (T-5): KULISH VIKTORIIA/Shutterstock; p.33 (CL): American Spirit/Shutterstock; p.33 (C): View Pictures/Getty Images; p.33 (CR): Elnur/Shutterstock; p.33 (BL): Sergio Bertino/Shutterstock; p.33 (BC): Styve Reineck/Shutterstock; p.34 (TL): Denis Radovanovic/Shutterstock; p.34 (TR): Michael DeYoung/Blend Images/Corbis; p.34 (CL): Pictorium/Alamy; p.34 (BR): tab62/Shutterstock; p.36–37: Simon GRATIEN/Getty Images; p.39 (a), p.41 (BC), p.84 (CR): Monkey Business Images/Shutterstock; p.39 (b): StockLite/Shutterstock; p.39 (c): Juice Images/Alamy; p.39 (d): Horizons WWP/Alamy; p.41 (B/G): fototrav/Getty Images; p.41 (TL): v.s.anandhakrishna/Shutterstock; p.41 (TC): Byelikova Oksana/Shutterstock; p.41 (TR): Lumi images/Alamy; p.41 (BL): holbox/Shutterstock; p.41 (BR): Klaus Vedfelt/Getty Images; p.43 (BR): Rainer von Brandis/Getty Images; p.44: Tom Bean/Alamy; p.45 (T-1): Grzegorz Petrykowski/Shutterstock; p.45 (T-2): Leandro Mise/Alamy; p.45 (T-3): Lloyd Sutton/Alamy; p.45 (T-4): RosalreneBetancourt5/Alamy; p.45 (CL): David R. Frazier Photolibrary, Inc./Alamy; p.45 (CR): Nature Picture Library/Alamy; p.45 (BL): ITAR-TASS Photo Agency/Alamy; p.45 (BC): Steve Arnold/Alamy; p.46–47: Thomas Marent/Minden Pictures/Corbis; p.50 (1): Dirk Ercken/Shutterstock; p.50 (2): Milosz_M/Shutterstock; p.50 (4): JI de Wet/Shutterstock; p.50 (BL): Ryan M. Bolton/Shutterstock; p.50 (BC-penguin): Anton_Ivanov/Shutterstock; p.50 (BC-rabbit): Andrew Parkinson/Corbis; p.50 (BR): Louise Murray/Robert Harding World Imagery/Corbis; p.51 (B/G): Subbotina Anna/Shutterstock; p.51 (B/G-inset): Oli Scarff/Getty Images; p.51 (a): Miso Lisanin/Xinhua Press/Corbis; p.51 (b): Gerry Pearce/Alamy; p.51 (c): frans lemmens/Alamy; p.53 (B/G), p.75 (B/G): SZE FEI WONG/Getty Images; p.53 (BR): Cathy Keifer/Shutterstock; p.54: Thomas Dressier/Getty Images; p.55 (1-TL): Ricardo Canino/Shutterstock; p.55 (1-TR): Johan Swanepoel/Shutterstock; p.55 (2-TL): subin pumsom/Shutterstock; p.55 (2-TR): Matt Jeppson/Shutterstock; p.55 (3-TL): reptiles4all/Shutterstock; p.55 (CL): Bill Kennedy/Shutterstock; p.55 (C): Dirk Ercken/Shutterstock; p.55 (CR): Audrey Snider-Bell/Shutterstock; p.55 (BL): Mikadun/Shutterstock; p.55 (BC): Jean-Edouard Rozey/Shutterstock; p.56 (TL): C Flanigan/FilmMagic/Getty Images; p.56 (TR): Hugo Ortuno Suarez/Getty Images; p.56 (BL): Stock Connection Blue/Alamy; p.56 (BR), p.89 (TL): Hemis/Alamy; p.58–59: Richard Rudisill/Getty Images; p.62 (salad): Nitr/Shutterstock; p.62 (toast): triocean/Shutterstock; p.62 (burger): page frederique/Shutterstock; p.62 (ice cream): M. Unal Ozmen/Shutterstock; p.62 (fruit): Lestertair/Shutterstock; p.62 (veg), p.77 (BL): Africa Studio/Shutterstock; p.62 (sandwich): Food and Drink Photos/Alamy; p.62 (chicken): papkin/Shutterstock; p.62 (pasta): marmo81/Shutterstock; p.62 (fish): TAGSTOCK1/Shutterstock; p.62 (nuts): Suprun Vitaly/Shutterstock; p.62 (yoghurt): nito/Shutterstock; p.63 (B/G): Marina Grau/Shutterstock; p.63 (TL): TS/Alamy; p.63 (CL): sanneberg/Shutterstock; p.63 (BR): David Papazian/Corbis; p.65 (BR): Nigel J. Dennis/Corbis; p.66: Paul Souders/Corbis; p.67 (T-1): sondem/Shutterstock; p.67 (T-2): Lex van Groningen/Buiten-beeld/Minden Pictures/Corbis; p.67 (T-3): Art Directors & TRIP/Alamy; p.67 (T-4): Denis Kichatof/Shutterstock; p.67 (CL): peresanz/Shutterstock; p.67 (CR), p.93 (BC-afternoon): imageBROKER/Alamy; p.67 (BL): Julian Love/JAI/Corbis; p.67 (BC): Dori Moreno/Getty Images; p.68–69: Hero Images/Getty Images; p.72 (1): Fabrice LEROUGE/Getty Images; p.72 (3): Bob Mitchell/Corbis; p.72 (a): Agencja Fotograficzna Caro/Alamy; p.72 (b): Michael Krasowitz/Getty Images; p.72 (c): Radius Images/Alamy; p.72 (d): BSIP SA/Alamy; p.73 (B/G): Irina Mos/Shutterstock; p.73 (B/G-inset): Malivan_Iuliia/Shutterstock; p.73 (BL): Klaus Vedfelt/Getty Images; p.75 (BR): Chris Cheadle/Alamy; p.76: Everything/Shutterstock; p.77 (1-TL): Destinyweddingstudio/Shutterstock; p.77 (1-TR): Mikhail Pozhenko/Shutterstock; p.77 (2-TL): Denis Tabler/Shutterstock; p.77 (2-TR): tristan tan/Shutterstock; p.77 (3-TL): Gallo Images/Alamy; p.77 (3-TR): Antonova Anna/Shutterstock; p.77 (CL): John Elk III/Getty Images; p.77 (C): Elly Godfroy/Alamy; p.77 (CR): Alexandr Makarov/Shutterstock; p.77 (BC): my nordic/Shutterstock; p.78 (TL): Brachat, Oliver/the4 food passionates/Corbis; p.78 (TR): 2/Andersen Ross/Ocean/Corbis; p.78 (BL): Bloomimage/Corbis; p.78 (BR): Food Centrale Hamburg GmbH/Alamy; p.80–81: Krzysztof Dydynski/Getty Images; p.83 (John): Jupiterimages/Getty Images; p.83 (Marta): kali9/Getty Images; p.83 (Leon): David Burton/Alamy; p.84 (CL): Khakimullin Aleksandr/Shutterstock; p.84 (B): Christian Mueller/Shutterstock; p.85 (B/G): balabolka/Shutterstock; p.85 (TL): Andre Babiak/Alamy; p.85 (BL): dwphotos/Shutterstock; p.87 (BR): KathyKafka/Getty Images; p.88: Sasa Komien/Shutterstock; p.89 (TR): Pecold/Shutterstock; p.89 (TC): ARCTIC IMAGES/Alamy; p.89 (CL): saras66/Shutterstock; p.89 (CR): kosmos111/Shutterstock; p.89 (BL): Evgeny Prokofyev/Getty Images; p.89 (BC): David South/Alamy; p.89 (BR-inset): Noradoa/Shutterstock; p.90–91: All Canada Photos/Alamy; p.93 (BL): shotstock/Alamy; p.93 (BC-evening): p.93 (BR): Cal Vornberger/Alamy; p.95 (B/G): nodff/Shutterstock; p.95 (a): JTB MEDIA CREATION, Inc/Alamy; p.95 (b): stock_shot/Shutterstock; p.95 (c): Ulana Switucha/Alamy; p.95 (d): wisarut_ch/Shutterstock; p.97 (BR): MIKEL BILBAO GOROSTIAGA-NATURE & LANDSCAPES/Alamy; p.98: Wan Ru Chen/Getty Images; p.99 (T-1): Mike Hill/Alamy; p.99 (T-2): Cultura Science/Jason Persoff Stormdoctor/Getty Images; p.99 (T-3): epa european pressphoto agency b.v./Alamy; p.99 (T-4): Petri Artturi Asikinen/Getty Images; p.99 (T-5): Australian Land, City, People Scape Photographer/Getty Images; p.99 (CL): Aaron Horowitz/Corbis; p.99 (C): peresanz/Shutterstock; p.99 (CR): Jim Reed/Jim Reed Photography – Severe&/Corbis; p.99 (BL): Gregory Pelt/Shutterstock; p.99 (BC): Igumnova Irina/Shutterstock; p.100 (TL): Adrian Sherratt/Alamy; p.100 (TR): Golden Pixels LLC/Alamy; p.100 (BL): Stockbyte/Getty Images; p.100 (BR): benedektibor/Getty Images; p.102 (B/G), p.103 (B/G): blue67design/Shutterstock; p.102 (T), p.102 (C), p.102 (BR), p.103 (T), p.103 (CR), p.103 (BL), p.103 (BR): Elena Schweitzer/Shutterstock.

Commissioned photography by Gareth Boden: p.11 (T); p.13 (BR); p.18 (T); p.21 (T); p.23 (BR); p.31 (T); p.33 (BR); p.40 (T); p.43 (T); p.45 (BR); p.50 (T); p.53 (T); p.55 (BR); p.62 (T); p.65 (T); p.67 (BR); p.71 (B); p.72 (T); p.72 (2); p.72 (4); p.73 (a–d); p.75 (T); p.77 (BR); p.84 (T); p.87 (T); p.89 (BR); p.94 (T); p.97 (T); p.99 (BR)

Our special thanks to the following for their kind help during location photography:

Queen Emma Primary School

Front Cover photo by Gerardo Ricardo Lopez/Getty Images